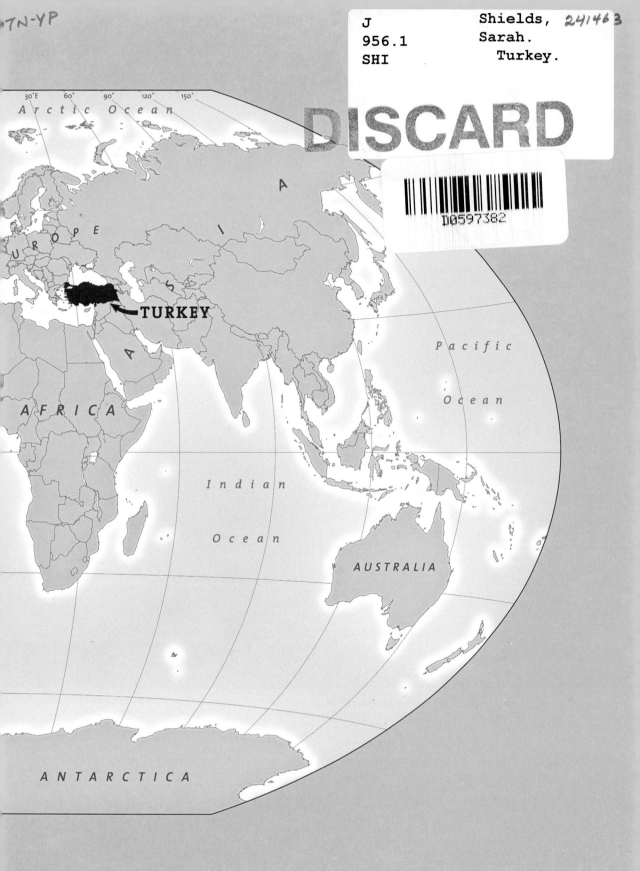

Arctic Ocean

30°E 60° 90° 120° 150°

A S I A

EUROPE

AFRICA

TURKEY

Pacific

Ocean

Indian

Ocean

AUSTRALIA

ANTARCTICA

Turkey

Sarah Shields

Michael A. McAdams and Allison Hart, Consultants

NATIONAL GEOGRAPHIC

WASHINGTON, D.C.

Contents

4 Foreword

7 GEOGRAPHY

The Land of the Cotton Castle

8 At a Glance

> What's the Weather Like?

> Fast Facts

> Average Temperature & Rainfall

> Physical Map

10 Special Feature: Half-Dead and Dangerous

11 Special Feature: Straits and Narrows

12 Special Feature: Unsteady Ground

15 Special Feature: Noah's Mountain

17 NATURE

A Haven for Birds

18 At a Glance

> Turkey Red

> Species at Risk

> Vegetation & Ecosystems Map

20 Special Feature: Big Dogs for Big Cats

22 Special Feature: Fields of Flowers

25 HISTORY

Center of Civilizations

26 At a Glance

> An Ancient Civilization

> Time line

> Historical Map

28 Special Feature: The Midas Touch

29 Special Feature: Ancient Wonder

30 Special Feature: Life Underground

32 Special Feature: A City on Two Continents

35 Special Feature: Atatürk: Father Turk

37 PEOPLE & CULTURE
A Hospitable Mix

38 At a Glance
  > Urban and Rural Population
  > Common Turkish Phrases
  > Population Map

41 Special Feature: National Holidays

42 Special Feature: The Blue Mosque

43 Special Feature: Dervishes

44 Special Feature: Leading Writer

46 Special Feature: Sports Fans

49 GOVERNMENT & ECONOMY
Ancient but Modern

50 At a Glance
  > Government and Religion
  > Trading Partners
  > Political Map

52 Special Feature: How the Government Works

53 Special Feature: Minority Voices

54 Special Feature: Europe: In or Out?

55 Special Feature: Nuts about Nuts

56 Special Feature Map: Industry

58 Add a Little Extra to Your Country Report!

60 Glossary

61 Bibliography
  Further Information

62 Index

64 Credits

Foreword

What do you think of when you imagine Turkey? Some people might envision the bazaars of Istanbul, lined with colorful carpets and leather goods. Others' thoughts might go to the grand architecture of Hagia Sofia, the Topkapi Palace, or the ancient sites of Ephesus and Troy. Whatever first comes to mind, the vision likely hints at the mixture of cultures and times that mark Turkey as the great connector of East and West.

For thousands of years Turkey has served as a bridge between cultures and as home to civilizations. Byzantium of old became Constantinople, seat of the Eastern Roman or Byzantine Empire and home of the Orthodox Christian church for centuries. Later, Constantinople became Istanbul, the capital of the Ottoman Empire and seat of the Islamic caliphate. With changes in power came shifts in culture. Populations mixed and traditions blended. Turkey today is the product of these and other influences.

This book offers a glimpse into the people and cultures that have shaped Turkey's history, the landscape that has set the stage, and the natural resources that have encouraged people to traverse and settle on this strategic piece of land for many centuries. But this volume not only looks back at what Turkey has been. It also sheds light on what the country is today: a vibrant democracy in a place that is as much a crossroads between two cultures as it was two thousand years ago.

With so many influences and so many changes over time, it is no wonder that Turkey is still working to find its identity. The people take great pride in being Turkish, but they are still trying to define what exactly that means, especially for the people who come from other ethnic back-

grounds, like the Kurds. The majority of Turkey's population is Muslim, and at the same time the country is committed to keeping religion out of public life.

Today, as so many times before, Turkey's position between East and West makes its role in the world an important one. Turkey is part of the West—a member of the military alliance, NATO, and a potential member of the European Union. It borders several energy-rich states and has the potential to act as an important transit route for the energy resources needed in Europe and elsewhere. Looking east, Turkey serves as an example to the Middle East as the most advanced democracy in the Muslim world. For these reasons and others, Turkey is an important and fascinating country to which this book provides an excellent introduction.

▲ Istanbul, the Turkish capital, rises beside the Golden Horn, an inlet of the Bosporus. A city has stood on the narrow waterway for three thousand years.

Allison Hart
The Brookings Institution,
Washington, D.C.

The Land of the Cotton Castle

MOST PEOPLE ARE ASTONISHED when they see the cliffs at Pamukkale in western Turkey. From a distance, it looks as if a sheet of ice is covering the hillside. A closer look reveals pools of water in a series of ledges. The white cliffs are not made of ice but of a calcium-rich mineral called travertine. As spring water trickles from pool to pool, it leaves behind crystals of travertine, gradually adding to the 1.7-mile (2.7 km) long cascade.

Ancient people named the cliff the Cotton Castle. They thought the waters could heal the sick and built baths and temples around the hot springs at the top of the cliff. The Romans thought that a cave up there was a gateway to the underworld. Anyone who went in never came out—they were probably killed by poison gases.

◄ **Pamukkale is one of Turkey's top tourist attractions. People once bathed in the warm pools, but climbing on the rocks is now forbidden to protect the site.**

WHAT'S THE WEATHER LIKE?

Turkey's mountains and long coastlines create weather conditions that vary widely in different parts of the country. Cities near the sea have a mild climate. The northern coast, along the Black Sea, gets the most rain. The mountains that skirt Turkey's coasts stop most of the rain from reaching inland. As a result the south is almost a desert. As well as being dry, Turkey's inland areas have hotter summers and colder winters than the coasts. Snow covers the eastern mountains for as long as four months a year.

The map opposite shows the physical features of Turkey. Labels on this map and on similar maps throughout this book identify most of the places pictured in each chapter.

MAP KEY
Dry
Semiarid
Mild
Mediterranean

Black Sea

Mediterranean Sea

0   mi   200
0   km   200

Fast Facts

OFFICIAL NAME: Republic of Turkey

FORM OF GOVERNMENT: Parliamentary democracy

CAPITAL: Ankara

POPULATION: 73,884,000

OFFICIAL LANGUAGE: Turkish

CURRENCY: Turkish lira

AREA: 302,535 square miles (783,562 square kilometers)

BORDERING NATIONS: Armenia, Azerbaijan, Bulgaria, Georgia, Greece, Iran, Iraq, Syria.

HIGHEST POINT: Great Ararat, 16,945 feet (5,165 meters)

LOWEST POINT: Sea level, 0 feet (0 meters)

MAJOR MOUNTAIN RANGES: Taurus Mountains, Eastern Anatolian Highlands

MAJOR RIVERS: Euphrates, Tigris, Sakarya, Kizil, Ceyhan, Seyhan, Yenice

MAJOR LAKES: Lake Van, Tuz Lake

COASTLINE: 4,474 miles (7,207 kilometers)

Average Temperature & Rainfall

Average High/Low Temperatures; Yearly Rainfall

ISTANBUL (WEST): 65° F (19° C) / 50° F (10° C); 25 in (62 cm)

ANTALYA (SOUTH): 75° F (24° C) / 56° F (13° C); 41 in (105 cm)

ANKARA (CENTER): 61° F (16° C) / 41° F (5° C); 18 in (45 cm)

TRABZON (NORTH): 64° F (18° C) / 53° F (12° C); 32 in (80 cm)

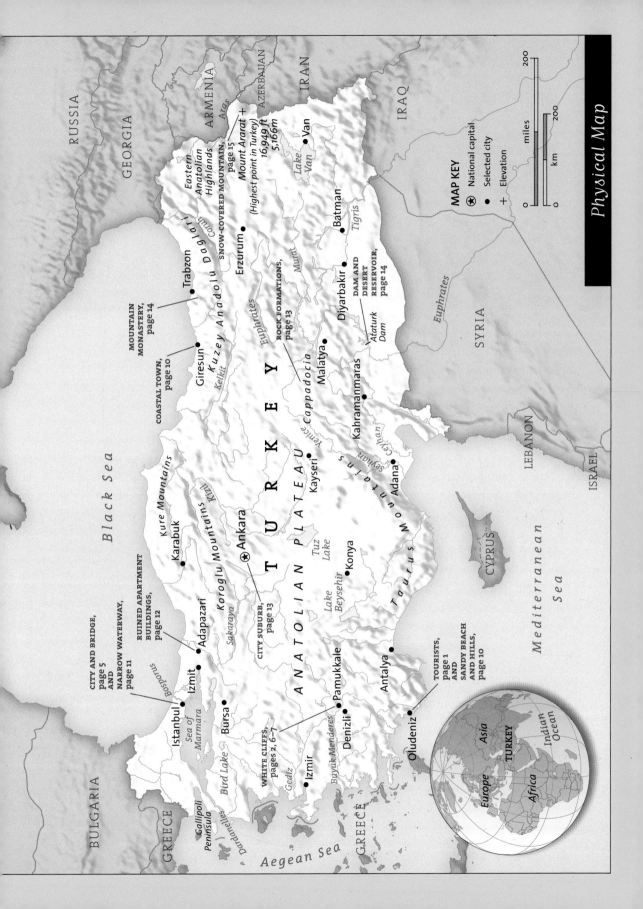

Physical Map

RUSSIA

GEORGIA

ARMENIA

AZERBAIJAN

Aras

IRAN

IRAQ

SYRIA

LEBANON

ISRAEL

*Eastern
Anatolian
Highlands*

Coruh

**SNOW-COVERED MOUNTAIN,
page 15**

Mount Ararat +
16,949 ft
5,166m
(Highest point in Turkey)

Lake
Van • Van

Trabzon

Kuzey Anadolu Dağları

Erzurum

Batman

Kelkit

Tigris

Euphrates

**MOUNTAIN
MONASTERY,
page 14**

**COASTAL TOWN,
page 10**

Giresun

**ROCK FORMATIONS,
page 13**

Murat

Diyarbakir

**DAM AND
DESERT
RESERVOIR,
page 14**

Ataturk
Dam

Euphrates

Cappadocia

T U R K E Y

Malatya

Kahramanmaras

Yentce

Ceyhan

Kayseri

Sultan Mountains

Adana

Seyhan

**CITY AND BRIDGE,
page 5
AND
NARROW WATERWAY,
page 11**

**RUINED APARTMENT
BUILDINGS,
page 12**

Kure Mountains

Karabuk

A N A T O L I A N   P L A T E A U

Ankara

Koroglu Mountains

Kızıl

*Tuz
Lake*

Konya

Taurus Mountains

Sakarya

Adapazari

**CITY SUBURB,
page 13**

*Lake
Beysehir*

Black Sea

Izmit

Bosporus

Istanbul

*Sea of
Marmara*

Bursa

Bird Lake

Pamukkale

Antalya

**TOURISTS,
page 1
AND
SANDY BEACH
AND HILLS,
page 10**

Oludeniz

CYPRUS

Mediterranean
Sea

BULGARIA

GREECE

*Gallipoli
Peninsula*

Dardanelles

GREECE

Gediz

Izmir

Buyuk Menderes

Denizli

**WHITE CLIFFS,
pages 2, 6–7**

Aegean Sea

MAP KEY

⊛ National capital
• Selected city
+ Elevation

miles

km

0   200

0   200

Europe

Asia

Africa

TURKEY

Indian
Ocean

▲ The beach at Olüdeniz on Turkey's Aegean coast is regarded as the most beautiful in the country.

A Country in Two Continents

Turkey is one of the few countries of the world that serve as a bridge between two continents: Europe and Asia. Turkey is thought to be one of the first places on Earth where humans lived in towns, farmed crops, and made metal tools. In the many centuries since then,

HALF-DEAD AND DANGEROUS

The Black Sea north of Turkey is an unusual body of water. It may be named for the black sand of its beaches, or its name may reflect its stormy conditions. In ancient times, it was known as the "Inhospitable Sea." If it were not for a single strait connecting it to the Mediterranean Sea, the Black Sea would be the world's biggest lake. Being far from the open ocean, the Black Sea's water is not mixed by strong currents. It is only half as salty as ocean water. Although the upper levels of the sea are full of fish, virtually nothing lives in the deepest parts of the Black Sea. No oxygen or nutrients circulate down there to support living things.

▲ The city of Giresun is on the hilly eastern Black Sea coast.

STRAITS AND NARROWS

▲ A container ship travels along the Bosporus and through the heart of Istanbul.

European Turkey is divided from the Asian part by the Sea of Marmara. This is a wide strait that connects the Black Sea to the Mediterranean. Ships traveling through the Sea of Marmara must pass through two narrow waterways at either end. To the south the Dardanelles connect with the Mediterranean. The Dardanelles run for 31 miles (68 km) between the rocky Gallipoli peninsula and the mainland. To the north, the Bosporus leads to the Black Sea. The 19-mile (30 km) Bosporus (Bogaz, or "neck," in Turkish) runs right through the middle of Istanbul. It is a dangerous waterway. It has two currents; one at the surface goes north, but another deeper down moves in the opposite direction. Many ships have crashed trying to steer the winding route in the currents.

The two waterways are important shipping routes. For example, they are the only way ships can reach the ports of southern Russia. Many wars have been fought over the narrows, including the Crimean War (1853–1856) and the Gallipoli campaign of World War I (1914–1918).

the country has been a stepping stone between Europe and Asia, and among the ancient civilizations of Greece, Rome, and Persia. Its geography makes it an important part of the trade routes between the two continents. As a result, it has often been fought over and settled. Modern Turkey is shaped by this wide range of influences.

Surrounded by Water

Most of Turkey is a huge peninsula, surrounded by water on three sides: the Black Sea to the north, the Mediterranean Sea to the south, and the Aegean Sea

UNSTEADY GROUND

Turkey is in one of the most active earthquake zones in the world. The North Anatolian Fault, which runs from the Sea of Marmara to the Eastern Anatolian Highlands, shudders back and forth up to 8 inches (20 cm) a year. In the past 70 years this part of the country has experienced 13 earthquakes. A total of about 55,000 people were killed during these disasters.

One of the largest quakes occurred in 1999 near Izmit, an industrial town about 55 miles (90 km) east of Istanbul. The quake measured 7.4 on the Richter Scale—tremors are rarely stronger than this. It struck at 3 A.M. and within

▲ Apartment buildings in Adapazari—a neighboring city to Izmit—fell down because the 1999 earthquake loosened the soil around their foundations.

48 seconds, at least 17,000 of Izmit's people were dead. The greatest cause of death was due to the poor construction of the city's buildings, which fell down as people slept inside.

(a small arm of the Mediterranean) to the west. Most of Turkey's land borders are to the east, where it meets Syria, Iraq, Iran, Azerbaijan, Armenia, and Georgia.

Turkey's only other neighbors—Greece and Bulgaria—are in the west. Here, the country occupies a narrow strip of European land, divided from the rest of Turkey by a set of narrow seaways: the Bosporus, the Sea of Marmara, and the Dardanelles.

Turkey's largest city, Istanbul, is built on the Bosporus and is partly in Europe and partly in Asia. Children living in Europe often "go to Asia" to see their grandparents, drinking orange juice on the ferries that cross the Bosporus every few minutes. Motorists

drive from one continent to the other across one of Istanbul's two Bosporus Bridges. A new rail tunnel being built beneath the Bosporus will soon carry commuters and freight between the continents. Construction often has to stop when the tunnelers find ancient archaeological remains.

A Corner of Asia

The Asian part of Turkey is a huge peninsula called Anatolia. This area is a little larger than the U.S. state of Texas. Western Anatolia is a fertile plateau and forms

▲ Ankara, the capital of Turkey, is the largest city on the Anatolian plateau.

▼ Unusual rock formations are found in Cappadocia in central Anatolia. The formations are made of hard rock left behind as softer rocks were eroded away.

the main farming region of Turkey. The Aegean coast in the west is also fertile, and grows olives and fruits. The beaches along this coast are a haven for tourists.

High and Dry

Eastern Anatolia is more mountainous. The Eastern Anatolian Highlands cover the northeast and spread out of Turkey to connect with the larger Caucasus Range. Turkey's longest range, the Taurus Mountains, runs from the south coast to the eastern border.

The southeastern foothills of the Taurus Mountains are home to Kurdish people, who speak their own language as well as Turkish. There are also small groups of Arabic-speaking Turks. This is the poorest part of Turkey. Its cities are still relatively small.

▲ A monastery clings to the side of a wooded mountain in northeastern Turkey.

▼ Atatürk Dam was built across the Euphrates River in 1992 to provide electricity and fresh water to southeast Turkey.

NOAH'S MOUNTAIN

Turkey's highest peak, Mount Ararat, is in the far east of the country in the Eastern Anatolian Highlands. The mountain overlooks Turkey's borders with Armenia and Iran. The mountain has two peaks, both of which are extinct volcanoes. Little Ararat is about 7 miles (II km) to the east of Great Ararat, which rises 16,945 feet (5,165 m). The Turkish name for the tallest peak is Ari Dai, meaning Mountain of Pain. The local Kurdish-speaking people call it the Mountain of Fire.

Mount Ararat is considered to be sacred by many different people. According to the Old Testament, it is where Noah landed his ark after the Great Flood. According to tradition, Noah built an altar on the mountain. However the village and monastery built at that spot were destroyed by an earthquake and avalanche in 1840. In separate Armenian and Persian legends, Mount Ararat is the birthplace of the first humans.

▲ Mount Ararat is covered in snow all year round, but the region around it is still one of the driest in Turkey.

The countryside is too dry for growing crops. The country's largest lake, Lake Van, is located there, but its water is too salty to be used for irrigating the soil. However, the Taurus Mountains are the source of the two largest rivers in the Middle East—the Tigris and Euphrates, which in Turkish are called the Dicle and the Firat. These rivers carry the meltwater from the mountains southward all the way to the Persian Gulf. The river systems are now being dammed to provide water and electricity and give the region a much-needed boost.

A *Haven for Birds*

TURKEY IS AN IMPORTANT STOP on the routes that migrating birds take between their summer and winter homes. Birds prefer to fly over land than over sea, so many birds traveling back and forth between Europe and Africa take the eastern route around the Mediterranean through Turkey.

Each spring and fall thousands of birds take a rest around Turkey's marshlands and lakes. As its name suggests, Kus Golu, or Bird Lake, is one such place. The shallow lake is in one of Turkey's protected national forests. It is surrounded by reed marshes that are fed by flood waters from the lake. Together, the different habitats provide homes for more than 270 species of birds, including various kinds of ducks, geese, pygmy cormorants, and blue herons.

◄ **A fisherman passes a flock of pelicans on Bird Lake. The birds will spend winter on the lake and fly back to Russia in spring.**

TURKEY RED

Historians think that grain farming began in Anatolia and the surrounding areas, when people stopped collecting the seeds of wild grasses and learned how to grow wheat and other crops. Much of the bread North Americans eat is made partly from a breed of wheat called Turkey Red. The seeds were brought from the Black Sea region by immigrants to the United States in the late 1800s. Turkey Red quickly became the most common wheat in the American Midwest.

Wheat is not the only well-known plant that spread to the rest of the world from Turkey. Turkey has more than 9,000 species of wildflowers. Many cut flowers, such as tulips and roses, that are now popular across the world were originally wildflowers in eastern Turkey. The map opposite shows the vegetation zones—or what grows where—in Turkey.

Species at Risk

The first Turkish national park was opened in 1958. Today there are a total of 39. The parks protect rare species and habitats, highlight beautiful wilderness, and also contain many important historic sites.

Species at risk include:

> Dalmatian pelican
> Euphrates jerboa
  (rodent)
> Giant sturgeon (fish)
> Goitered gazelle
> Lesser kestrel
> Lycian salamander
> Mediterranean monk seal
> Mouflon (sheep)
> Red-breasted goose

▼ The northern bald ibis, also called the waldrap, is a critically endangered species. One of the few places these insect-eating birds survive is the dry hills of southern Turkey.

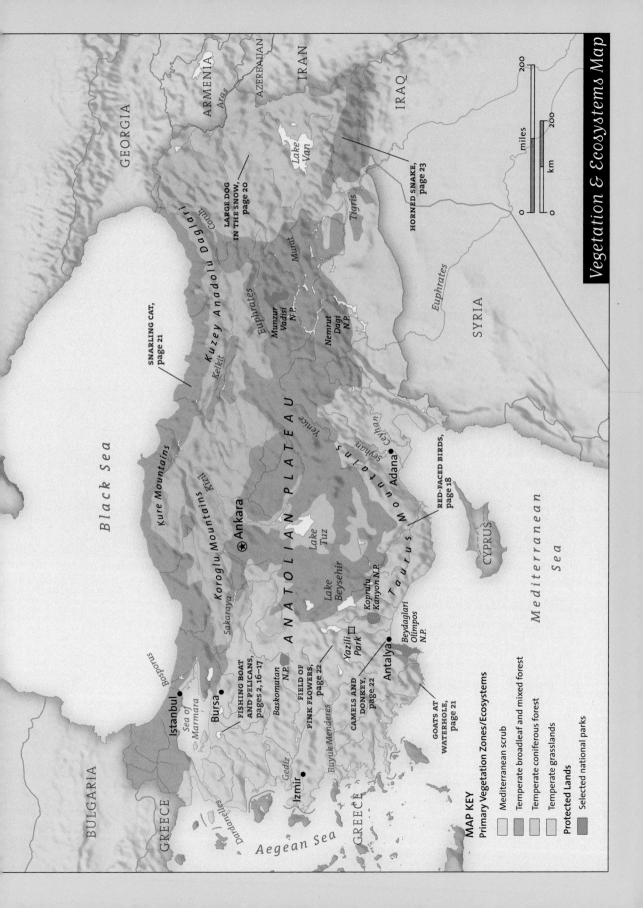

Vegetation & Ecosystems Map

BULGARIA

GREECE

GEORGIA

ARMENIA

AZERBAIJAN

IRAN

IRAQ

SYRIA

CYPRUS

GREECE

Black Sea

Sea of Marmara

Aegean Sea

Mediterranean Sea

Istanbul

Bursa

Izmir

Antalya

Adana

⊛ Ankara

Lake Van

Lake Tuz

Lake Beysehir

Bosporus

Dardanelles

Gediz

Buyuk Menderes

Sakarya

Kizil

Kelkit

Coruh

Aras

Murat

Euphrates

Euphrates

Tigris

Yenice

Seyhan

Ceyhan

Kure Mountains

Koroglu Mountains

Kuzey Anadolu Daglari

A N A T O L I A N   P L A T E A U

Taurus Mountains

SNARLING CAT, page 21

LARGE DOG IN THE SNOW, page 20

HORNED SNAKE, page 23

Munzur Vadisi N.P.

Nemrut Dagi N.P.

RED-FACED BIRDS, page 18

Baskomutan N.P.

Koprulu Kanyon N.P.

Beydaglari Olimpos N.P.

Nazili Park

FISHING BOAT AND PELICANS, pages 2, 16–17

FIELD OF PINK FLOWERS, page 22

CAMELS AND DONKEY, page 22

GOATS AT WATERHOLE, page 21

MAP KEY

Primary Vegetation Zones/Ecosystems

Mediterranean scrub

Temperate broadleaf and mixed forest

Temperate coniferous forest

Temperate grasslands

Protected Lands

Selected national parks

miles   0   200

km   0   200

Natural Crossroads

Turkey's history has been governed by the way it links Europe and Asia, and its natural history is no different. Some of the country's plants and animals are typical of the Mediterranean region while others are related to wildlife found in the Middle East.

There are two main types of habitat in Turkey. The central and southeastern parts of the country are generally too dry for trees to grow. Instead the landscape is covered in steppe, or grassland. Forests and woodland is the natural habitat of the rest of the country. However, people have lived in Turkey for so many centuries that most of the forests and other

BIG DOGS FOR BIG CATS

The kangal is the most famous Turkish breed of dog. For centuries, these dogs have been kept by farmers to protect their herds of sheep and goats from predators. The dogs have black heads and yellow bodies and they are large—males weighing as much as 155 pounds (70 kg). Kangals needed to be large to fight off attacking packs of wolves.

Wolves are very rare in modern Turkey but kangals are still common companions for shepherds. Some people have tried to make them family pets, because they bond so well with people and protect children and households. But kangals need a lot of room to run and prefer to be busy all day.

▲ The kangal is also known as the Anatolian shepherd dog.

Recently, people in Namibia have begun breeding Turkish kangals to protect animal herds from cheetahs. Farmers often shoot cheetahs for killing their animals. As a result the cats are now rare in Namibia. People hope that the kangals will scare away cheetahs, forcing them to hunt wild animals. Then Namibia's farmers will not shoot so many of the cats.

natural vegetation have been transformed into fields or pastures or are regularly harvested for lumber.

Trees Galore

The lushest forests are in the mountains along the eastern Black Sea coast, where rain falls at all times of year. The trees in these forests include sweet chestnut, oriental spruce, and alder. These green forests contrast with the drier woodlands in the west of Turkey, which contain small oaks, juniper trees, and pines.

Animals Come and Go

Turkey is home to many animal species, including bears, wolves, lynx, and jackals—although most of these are now rare. In the early 20th century, Turkey even had a population of tigers, an animal normally

▲ The forest cat is the wild relative of house cats. Turkey was one of the first places where cats were kept as pets.

▼ A herd of goats gathers around a waterhole in western Turkey.

FIELDS OF FLOWERS

The Turks love flowers, and many famous types were first cultivated in their country. The eastern mountains are home to many species of orchids, roses, and carnations. Tulips come from this same region. Small wild tulips were transported to Europe centuries ago. Years of breeding have resulted in the wealth of colors and shapes now admired worldwide. The lake region of Turkey has made garden roses into a big industry. This district in the center of Turkey has special shops that sell locally produced rose water, rose jam, rose cosmetics, and even rose-flavored candy.

According to Turkish tradition, tulips, roses, and carnations have special meanings. Artists use them to represent religious ideas. They were often included on the tiles that decorate mosques and palaces.

▲ Roses grow in a plantation on the western hills of the Taurus Mountains. The flowers are harvested for making perfumed oil and water.

▼ Camels can still be seen in the dry regions of southern Turkey, although they are becoming less common.

found in South and East Asia. The last Caspian tiger in Turkey was shot in 1970.

Turkey's three seas are a haven for fish, which provide a valuable source of food. But not all Turkey's sea life is faring so well. Several of the long sandy beaches on Turkey's Aegean coast are used by loggerhead turtles to lay their eggs. There are few suitable beaches left because tourists, who are also attracted to the golden sands, scare the turtles away. Turkey's Mediterranean monk seal is also at risk of extinction due to pollution.

Dolphins live in all the seas around Turkey. In fact, the sea mammals are a relatively common sight in Istanbul as they travel along the Bosporus. Sometimes dolphins stay awhile in the city's waters swimming into the Golden Horn, a long, narrow inlet that cuts through the European part of the city.

▲ Turbot and many other types of fish live in the waters that surround Turkey.

A Rich Blend

The Turkish government has set up many national parks and reserves. In a country like Turkey it is impossible to separate the natural world from its ancient human past. For example, hikers in the Yazili park in western Turkey can enjoy the mountain scenery as well as read the ancient Greek road signs carved on boulders. The trail through the park was once the main highway of the Persian Empire.

▼ The Turkish horned viper is named for the spike-like scales that poke up above its eyes.

Center
of
Civilizations

TURKEY'S LOCATION AT THE MEETING POINT of Europe and Asia and its rich resources have attracted many people to try to claim it for themselves. The modern country has been shaped by a complex and long history. Central Turkey was home to one of the earliest settlements in the world. Çatal Höyük was built 8,800 years ago. Excavations have revealed 13 different layers of buildings, each built on top of an earlier settlement. About 150 mud-brick houses were all joined together, with no streets between them. People entered through holes in the roofs. Between 5,000 and 8,000 people lived in the town. They decorated their buildings with murals and reliefs. Archaeologists have found many clay figurines of the mother-goddesses they worshipped.

◄ An archaeologist excavates obsidian artifacts in Çatal Höyük. The glassy black rock has sharp edges and was traded in the ancient world to make knives.

AN ANCIENT CIVILIZATION

Nearly 4,000 years ago, the Hittites established an empire centered in today's Anatolia. The Hittite empire captured territory south as far as Syria and battled with Egypt's King Ramses II. The Hittite civilization was based on worship of the sun goddess. Its craftspeople created gold jewelry, fine pottery, and graceful ironwork. The famous Trojan War, which is recounted in epics by the ancient poet Homer, took place as the Hittite empire was in decline in the late second millennium B.C. The probable site of Troy has been found at Hissarlik in northwest Anatolia.

▲ A modern statue at the ruins of Troy commemorates the legend that the Greeks smuggled warriors into the city hidden inside a wooden horse.

Time line

This chart shows the approximate dates of events in Turkey since 1750 B.C.

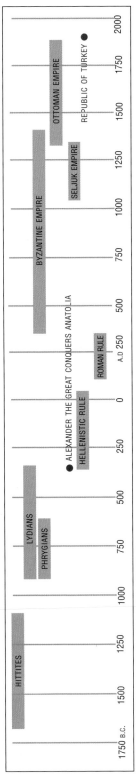

HITTITES

LYDIANS

PHRYGIANS

● ALEXANDER THE GREAT CONQUERS ANATOLIA

HELLENISTIC RULE

ROMAN RULE

BYZANTINE EMPIRE

SELJUK EMPIRE

OTTOMAN EMPIRE

REPUBLIC OF TURKEY ●

1750 B.C.　1500　1250　1000　750　500　250　0　A.D 250　500　750　1000　1250　1500　1750　2000

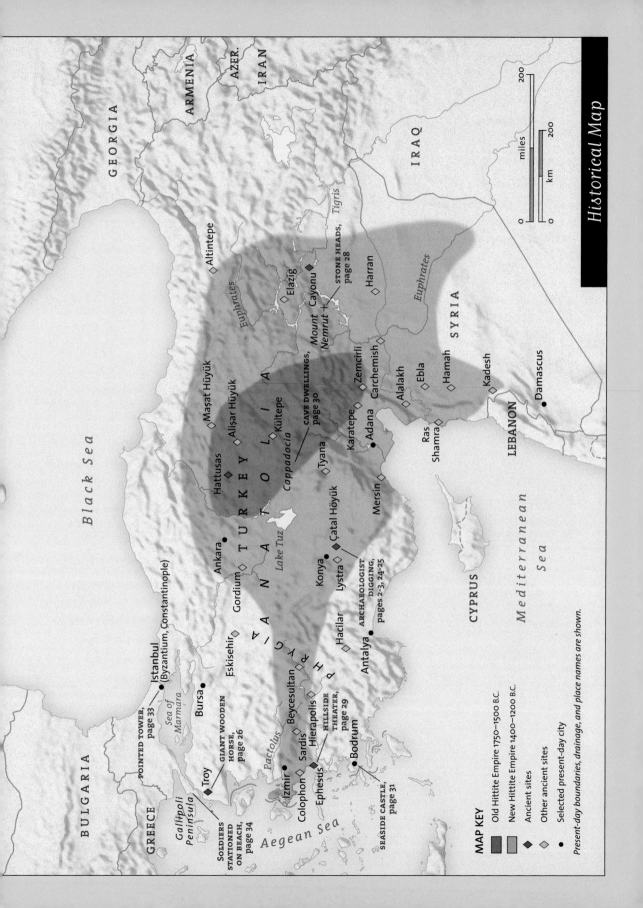

Historical Map

MAP KEY

Old Hittite Empire 1750–1500 B.C.

New Hittite Empire 1400–1200 B.C.

◆ Ancient sites

◇ Other ancient sites

• Selected present-day city

Present-day boundaries, drainage, and place names are shown.

0   200   miles
0   200   km

BULGARIA

GREECE

Galfipoli Peninsula

SOLDIERS STATIONED ON BEACH, page 34

Troy

GIANT WOODEN HORSE, page 26

POINTED TOWER, page 33

Istanbul (Byzantium, Constantinople)

Sea of Marmara

Bursa

Eskisehir

Ankara

GEORGIA

ARMENIA

AZER.

IRAN

Black Sea

TURKEY

ANATOLIA

Lake Tuz

Gordium

Altintepe

Maşat Hüyük

Alişar Hüyük

Hattusas

Kültepe

CAVE DWELLINGS, page 30

Cappadocia

Elazig

Cayonu

STONE HEADS, page 28

Mount Nemrut +

Euphrates

Euphrates

Tigris

Harran

Zemcirli

Carchemish

Tyana

Karatepe

Adana

SYRIA

Alalakh

Ebla

Hamah

Kadesh

Damascus

Ras Shamra

LEBANON

Konya

Çatal Höyük

Lystra

ARCHAEOLOGIST DIGGING, pages 2–3, 24–25

Hacilar

Mersin

Antalya

CYPRUS

Mediterranean Sea

PHRYGIA

Pactolus

Beycesultan

Sardis

Hierapolis

HILLSIDE THEATER, page 29

Colophon

Izmir

Ephesus

Bodrum

SEASIDE CASTLE, page 31

Aegean Sea

IRAQ

THE MIDAS TOUCH

In an ancient Greek myth, King Midas helped Silenus, companion of the god Dionysus. As his reward from the god, Midas wished that everything he touched would turn to gold. The king nearly starved when all his food turned to gold. Then, his daughter hugged him and turned into a gold statue. Dionysus allowed the king to wash off the curse by bathing in the Pactolus River. The story is a legend, but Midas was the name of a real king of Phrygia—an area in western Turkey. Midas traded with his neighbors and his name is recorded on monuments dating from about 700 B.C. The myth of Midas was used to explain the gold dust that was found in the mud of the Pactolus River. A century later, the Lydians who lived along the river used its precious metals to make the world's first coins.

Land of Kings

After the Hittite Empire disappeared in about 1100 B.C., many other groups ruled Anatolia. They included the Phrygians. Their most famous king was Midas. His story of greed is known around the world. Another wealthy Turkish king was Croesus, who ruled Lydia. This was the first civilization to make coins. To this day, enormously wealthy people are still said to be "as rich as Croesus."

People from what is now Greece began to settle in western Anatolia. The two cultures influenced each other. The people of Anatolia took up Greek traditions, but Greek culture also changed because of its contact with local civilizations. By 334 B.C., the Macedonian Greek leader Alexander

▼ The heads of giant statues litter the peak of Mount Nemrut in southeast Turkey. In the first century B.C. the statues stood 26 feet (8 m) tall around the tomb of Antiochus I, a king who ruled Syria and eastern Turkey.

ANCIENT WONDER

Ephesus began as a shrine to the goddess Cybele (later known as Artemis) but by 600 B.C. it was a busy port on the Aegean Sea. The city's temple to Artemis is counted as one of the Seven Wonders of the Ancient World. The huge building took 120 years to erect after the original temple burned down in 356 B.C., when Herostratus, a madman, destroyed the temple as a way of being famous forever.

▲ The Great Theater at Ephesus was built into the side of a hill. It can hold 25,000 people.

Over the centuries Ephesus's harbor kept filling up with sand. A Greek ruler built a new city to the west, closer to the sea. He flooded the old city to force people to move. In Roman times, a quarter million people lived in Ephesus. The apostle Paul preached there on his way to Rome. The Virgin Mary was said to have lived her last days in the hills above Ephesus.

The harbor continued to fill up with sand, however, and Ephesus was abandoned. Today Ephesus is 4.5 miles (7 km) from the sea, but its ruins suggest that it was once a wealthy place. The streets are lined with marble columns. Its library is still intact and had room for 12,000 scrolls.

the Great had conquered most of modern Turkey. After Alexander died, Anatolia was invaded from both the east and the west as one group after another tried to claim the territory.

World Religions

Anatolia became the Roman province of Asia Minor in 129 B.C. and got a break from the frequent invasions. Soon after the crucifixion of Jesus Christ, his supporters came to Anatolia to preach. Christianity grew quickly —but so did Roman efforts to stop people from following the new faith. However, when Constantine

LIFE UNDERGROUND

The mountains, canyons, and caves of Cappadocia in central Turkey were once a refuge for people fleeing persecution or unfriendly governments. The unique region was shaped into its rugged form thanks to its mix of hard and soft rocks. These were eroded away at different rates to form natural columns called fairy chimneys. People made use of the soft rocks by digging their homes into the cliffs. Over the centuries, generations have built entire cities underground. Cappadocia's cave buildings include some of the world's first churches,

▲ Visitors explore caves in Cappadocia at dusk.

built 1,700 years ago and decorated with colorful wall paintings.

became Roman emperor in A.D. 324, he protected the Christians. By this time, the western part of the Roman Empire was becoming weaker, while the eastern part of the empire was becoming stronger. Constantine needed a new capital that was nearer to the more prosperous, peaceful east. He chose the ancient city of Byzantium on the Bosporus. He renamed the city Nova Roma Constantinopolitana, which meant "New Rome and the City of Constantine." Later, the city became known simply as Constantinople. As Rome and the western empire collapsed, the eastern Roman Empire ruled from Constantinople grew stronger and was transformed into what would later be called by historians the Byzantine Empire. In the same way, the Christian Church also split in two. Catholics remained based in Rome, while the Orthodox Church was run from Constantinople.

In the seventh century A.D., a new religion emerged in Arabia: Islam. Muslims soon settled in eastern Anatolia. Muslim groups arrived both as invaders and as peaceful settlers, and brought their own arts, laws, and customs. Anatolia would become an important part of the Muslim world, which had first been centered on Damascus, in modern Syria, and later on Baghdad, in what is now Iraq.

Warriors on Horseback

In the 11th century, Seljuk nomads came from Central Asia to dominate the Muslim world. They spoke a language similar to modern Turkish, and had already converted to Islam. They created a huge empire that included much of today's Turkey. Seljuk ideas, poetry, and science still influence the world today.

▼ The castle at Bodrum was built by Crusaders called the Knights Hospitaller in the early 15th century.

A CITY ON TWO CONTINENTS

When the Roman emperor Constantine began building a new capital, the site he chose was already ancient. A smaller city had stood there for a thousand years: Byzantium. The site had a natural harbor and controlled the waterway between the Black Sea and the Mediterranean. It marked where Europe met Asia. Constantine named the city Constantinople and boasted that it would be the new Rome.

The city remained unconquered for 1,000 years. However, the Ottomans finally took the city in 1453. They called it both Constantinople and Istanbul, a nickname meaning "to the city." Istanbul became the official name after the proclamation of the Republic of Turkey. The Ottomans used the city's palaces and converted the churches into mosques.

In 1923, Ankara became the capital of the new Turkish Republic. However, Istanbul is still Turkey's biggest city. Its population is now 16 million, and the city districts spread many miles into both Europe and Asia.

▼ **This modern artist's re-creation shows the city walls of Constantinople as they appeared in the 14th century.**

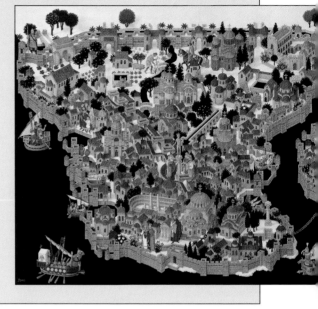

Later, the Seljuks began to fight among themselves. Eventually the empire divided into different Seljuk states. While Seljuk sultans fought against each other in the 12th century, Christian armies from Europe—known as Crusaders—took over much of western Asia, including parts of Turkey.

A Mighty Empire

In the 14th century there were many battles along the frontier between the Muslim and Christian worlds. One of the Muslim leaders attacking the Byzantine Empire was a nomad chief named Osman. His descendants, the Osmanlis or Ottomans, formed the mightiest army of the time. In 1453, Ottoman forces did the unthinkable—they took Constantinople. The city had been thought indestructible, because it was surrounded by water on three sides and guarded by huge walls.

Eventually the Ottoman Empire ruled not only Anatolia but also the Balkans as far as Vienna in Austria, and the whole Middle East from Algeria to the borders of Iran. For several centuries, the Ottoman Empire was the main power in the Middle East. It fought off attacks from Persia to the east and the Hapsburg Empire in the west.

▲ This portrait shows the Ottoman sultan Süleyman I.

Living Together

In peacetime, the Ottoman Empire was a hub of learning, art, and technology, centered on its vibrant capital, Istanbul. The great architect Sinan, for example, designed some of the most beautiful mosques ever

▼ The Galata Tower stands over northern Istanbul. It was built in 1348 by Constantinople's Italian community. The Galata district stayed neutral during the Ottoman invasion and was not incorporated into Istanbul until 1840.

built, such as the Süleyman Mosque in Constantinople. The empire contained a mix of peoples and cultures, with Christians, Muslims, and Jewish people all living together peacefully.

The sultan's power over his many peoples stemmed from his army. New recruits for the Ottoman army were collected by the *devshirme* system. Non-Muslim boys—mostly Christians from the Balkans—were taken from their families and raised as soldiers and sometimes government officials, or viziers. Most of these slave soldiers became Muslims. As a result, their own sons were exempt from devshirme.

▲ Allied troops unload supplies at Anzac Cove near Gallipoli in April 1915. Mustafa Kemal's Ottoman army stopped the invaders from reaching the Dardanelles. The Allies gave up and evacuated nine months later.

Empire's End

The Ottoman Empire finally ended in the years around World War I (1914–1918). Millions of Ottoman Muslims were forced to leave their homes as states emerged in the Balkans. Waves of immigrants arrived in Istanbul between 1912 and 1915. Peoples in Romania, Greece, and Bulgaria fought to establish their own nation-states. Defeat in World War I weakened the Ottoman Empire further. An army led by Mustafa Kemal fought to establish a Turkish nation-state in Anatolia.

As the Turks fought to establish their new country in the Turkish War of Independence (1919–1923),

ATATÜRK: FATHER TURK

Mustafa Kemal was born in 1881 in what is now Greece. He became an officer in the Ottoman army and, in World War I, led resistance to the Allied invasion at Gallipoli. When the empire was defeated, he refused to accept the terms of surrender. Instead, he led nationalists fighting the Greek, Italian, French, and British occupation of Anatolia. By 1923 the Turkish forces had won, and Mustafa Kemal became the leader of the Republic of Turkey. He insisted that the country reform itself and passed laws that changed the calendar, the alphabet, the role of religion, and even people's dress. He also demanded that all Turks take surnames. He took the last name Atatürk, or Father Turk.

civilians in the region were caught up in the conflict. Many Greeks and Armenians left the country, while many Muslim Greeks arrived. Mustafa Kemal became first president of the Republic of Turkey.

The Modern Republic

Mustafa Kemal insisted on making Turkey a secular country that would some day retake its place among the powers of the world. In the 80 years since the republic began, Turks have struggled over what their country should be like. Three times the army has taken control of the government to maintain order.

Today, Turkey is a democracy. Still, Turks continue to grapple with the questions that caused conflicts in the 20th century: What kind of democracy do we want? What should be the place of religion in our society? What do we want our country to be like?

A Hospitable Mix

SOCCER IS THE NATIONAL pastime in Turkey, and for Turkish fans the finals of Euro 2008 were unforgettable. Twice their team scored dramatic late goals to win key games. People poured into the streets of every town in Turkey to celebrate. In the semi-finals, Turkey faced its great rival, Germany. The two countries have close ties, but in the past the relationship was often uneven. About two million Turks live in Germany as guest workers. They began arriving in the early 1960s to take low-paid jobs because there was little work in Turkey. Since then, Turkey has grown more wealthy. It is on course to join Germany in the European Union. Turkey lost the soccer match, but in many ways Turks felt for the first time that the game was a meeting of equals.

◀ Turkish fans support their team during a game in the Euro 2008 tournament. The team got further than most people expected when it reached the semi-finals.

URBAN AND RURAL POPULATION

In 1927, three-quarters of Turkey's people lived in villages. Turkey then became steadily more industrialized, and more people found work in factories in cities. By the 1980s, almost two-thirds of Turks lived in cities. The number of people in the countryside has not gone down since 1987—it is still 24 million. However, the total population has increased.

The rapid growth of Turkey's population has strained resources. Schools are crowded, housing is harder to find, and roads and public transportation are under pressure. People who live in the countryside have the fewest public services. For example, a village child who wants to go to high school often has to move to a city.

▼ These girls belong to one of the few nomadic communities still living in Turkey. Their dress and lifestyle is similar to that of the original Ottomans and Seljuks.

Common Turkish Phrases

All Turks speak Turkish, which is related to the languages spoken in Central Asia. Some Turks also speak Arabic or Kurdish.

Hello	Merhaba (MER-ha-ba)
Good morning	Günaydin (gue-NAI-dein)
Good evening	Iyi aksamlar
	(e-AK-sham-lar)
Goodbye	Güle güle (GUE-le GUE-le)
Thank you	Tesekkür ederim
	(te-she-KUR ei-DER-eim)

1950 / 21 million	1970 / 36 million
22% urban / 78% rural	38% urban / 62% rural
1990 / 57 million	2005 / 73 million
59% urban / 41% rural	67% urban / 33% rural

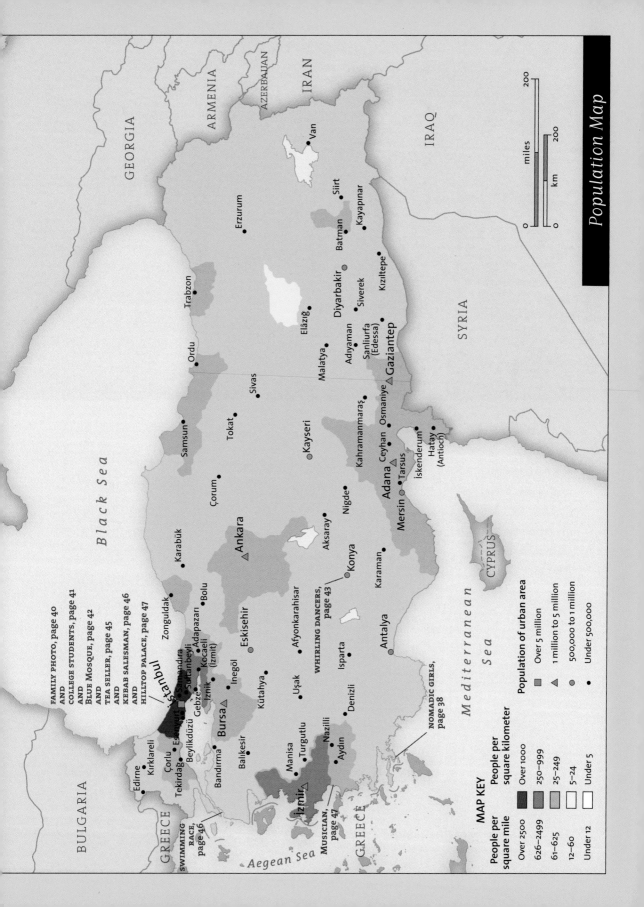

Population Map

MAP KEY

People per square mile

■ Over 2500	(darkest)
■ 626–2499	
■ 61–625	
□ 12–60	
□ Under 12	

People per square kilometer

■ Over 1000	
■ 250–999	
■ 25–249	
□ 5–24	
□ Under 5	

Population of urban area

■ Over 5 million	
▲ 1 million to 5 million	
● 500,000 to 1 million	
• Under 500,000	

Map scale
miles 0 — 200
km 0 — 200

Photo references
FAMILY PHOTO, page 40
AND
COLLEGE STUDENTS, page 41
AND
BLUE MOSQUE, page 42
AND
TEA SELLER, page 45
AND
KEBAB SALESMAN, page 46
AND
HILLTOP PALACE, page 47

SWIMMING RACE, page 46

MUSICIAN, page 47

WHIRLING DANCERS, page 43

NOMADIC GIRLS, page 38

Countries and Seas
BULGARIA
GREECE
GEORGIA
ARMENIA
AZERBAIJAN
IRAN
IRAQ
SYRIA
CYPRUS

Black Sea
Aegean Sea
Mediterranean Sea

Cities
Edirne
Kırklareli
Çorlu
Tekirdağ
İstanbul
Esenyurt
Beylikdüzü
Silivri
Çerkezköy
Adapazarı
Sultanbeyli
Gebze
Kocaeli (İzmit)
İznik
İnegöl
Bursa
Balıkesir
Bandırma
Manisa
Turgutlu
Nazilli
Aydın
İzmir
Uşak
Kütahya
Denizli
Isparta
Antalya
Karaman
Konya
Afyonkarahisar
Eskişehir
Bolu
Zonguldak
Karabük
Ankara
Aksaray
Niğde
Çorum
Tokat
Sivas
Kayseri
Kahramanmaraş
Osmaniye
Ceyhan
Adana
Tarsus
Mersin
İskenderum
Hatay (Antioch)
Gaziantep
Şanlıurfa (Edessa)
Adıyaman
Malatya
Elâzığ
Kızıltepe
Siverek
Diyarbakır
Kayapınar
Batman
Siirt
Elâzığ
Erzurum
Van
Ordu
Samsun
Trabzon

Extending the Family

"Happy is the person who calls himself a Turk" said
Turkey's first president, Atatürk. The quotation is
everywhere throughout the country, written on posters,
on statues, and even in huge letters on hillsides. But
just who are the Turks? According to the Turkish
government, Turks are the people who live within the
boundaries of Turkey and those who hold Turkish
passports even though they live abroad.

There are still many people living in Central Asia who
speak languages similar to Turkish. Historians believe
that the first Turkish-speaking people moved into
Anatolia from Central Asia centuries ago. Since then, all
the different groups who conquered Turkey left people
behind. A modern Turk is the descendant of many kinds

of people. Descendants of the Hittites mix with those of the Greeks and Romans. The Ottoman Empire included people from the Caucasus, the Balkans, and the Arab world, many of whom moved to live in what is now Turkey.

On the streets of Turkish cities, the mixing is clear: Turks look as if they come from everywhere. They sound as if they come from everywhere, too. There are many people in Turkey whose first language is not Turkish. Depending on where they live, they might speak Kurdish or Arabic at home. However, all children must learn to read and write in Turkish at school.

Diversity is also reflected in clothing. People dress differently around the country. Village women often wear scarves and their pants are baggy. In Turkey's cities, people dress much the same as they do in America. Some follow the latest fashions; others wear whatever is handy.

NATIONAL HOLIDAYS

Turkey's holidays mainly celebrate the creation of the republic. Other holidays are Muslim festivals, which are based on the Islamic calendar and move from year to year. The Sugar Holiday marks the end of the holy month of Ramadan. At the Festival of the Sacrifice Muslims remember Abraham's willingness to sacrifice his son Ishmael (known as Isaac to Christians). They sacrifice animals and give the meat to the poor. The holiday is also a time for family vacations.

NEW YEAR'S DAY	January 1
NATIONAL SOVEREIGNTY AND CHILDREN'S DAY	April 23
COMMEMORATION OF ATATÜRK, YOUTH, AND SPORTS DAY	May 19
VICTORY DAY	August 30
REPUBLIC DAY	October 29
RAMADAN BAYRAN (SUGAR HOLIDAY)	changes
FESTIVAL OF THE SACRIFICE	changes

▼ Students at Bogazici University in Istanbul reflect the wide mix of the Turkish people.

Religion in Turkey

Up to 97 percent of Turks are Muslim. Most are Sunni, belonging to the branch of Islam followed by most Muslims around the world. Many Turks are secular. Others are deeply religious. They pray five times a day, fast during the holy month of Ramadan, and try to model their lives on the Qur'an and the teachings of the Prophet Muhammad. The constitution makes religion a private matter. People are not allowed to bring religious symbols into schools or government offices. Recently, the Turkish Parliament has voted to allow women in universities and colleges to cover their heads with scarves, a common practice in Muslim culture. Some people see this as a sign that the government has become more tolerant. Others see it as a potentially dangerous threat to the principles of secularism.

THE BLUE MOSQUE

In the early 1600s, Sultan Ahmet I built a vast mosque in Istanbul. Although Turks call it the Sultan Ahmet Mosque, foreigners know it as the Blue Mosque. The name comes from the mosque's 20,000 handmade tiles from the city of Iznik. The tiles feature repeating patterns of mostly blue designs. Many include tulips.

Unlike other mosques, the Blue Mosque has six minarets, or towers, from which Muslims are called to prayer. At the time it was built, some people protested because the only other mosque in the world with six minarets was the Great Mosque in Mecca, in Saudi Arabia—the holiest place in Islam. Ahmet finally got permission to build six minarets in Istanbul after Muslim leaders decided to add a seventh tower to Mecca's important mosque.

▲ The six minarets of the Blue Mosque dominate the skyline in Istanbul.

DERVISHES

The Muslim mystic, or *sufi*, Jalal al-Din Rumi lived in Konya about 800 years ago. His writings are a spiritual guide for people seeking enlightenment. Even today, Rumi is a top-selling poet in the United States. Rumi's followers call him Mevlana, or "Our Guide." Rumi taught methods for feeling at one with all of God's creation. One way was using *sema*, or ritual turning. Mevlevis—the name for the Muslim sect that follow Rumi—became known as the Whirling Dervishes for their spinning dances. The word *dervish* comes from the Persian for "monk." In the 1920s, the Mevlevi sect was outlawed, but today it has won special status in Turkey. The dervishes now give performances around the world.

▲ Dervishes turn in long skirts that open out when spun.

Millions of Turks are Alevis. They share the Muslim belief in one God and in the prophecy of Muhammad. But Alevis have an inclusive faith that also includes beliefs from many world religions and traditional Anatolian culture from before the arrival of Islam.

The numbers of Christians and Jews in Turkey fell in the 20th century. However, an important leader of the Orthodox Church still lives in Istanbul. There are Armenian churches and schools, and small groups of Assyrians, Catholics, and Protestants are scattered around the country. Jews have lived in Anatolia since the fourth century B.C. The Ottoman Empire provided refuge for Jews fleeing the Spanish Inquisition in the 15th century, and again protected Jews fleeing from

LEADING WRITER

Orhan Pamuk (right) is Turkey's most famous living writer. He won the Nobel Prize for Literature in 2006. Pamuk writes novels about life in modern Turkey and the search for the country's soul. His most famous books in the West are his novels *The Black Book*, *My Name Is Red*, *Snow*, and his autobiography *Istanbul*. After he made a statement in 2005 about the Ottoman killings of Armenians in the 1910s, he faced criminal charges for "insulting Turkishness." The charges were dropped the next year.

the Nazis in the 20th century during World War II. Today, however, there are fewer than 50,000 Jews in the whole of Turkey, mostly living in Istanbul.

Family First

For Turks, family is very important. Young men and women usually live with their families until they go away to college or get married. Even then, they often find a place to live near their parents. Families get together regularly for dinners and holidays. Children may visit their cousins and grandparents on weekends.

Turkish children are required to go to school from age six to 14. After that, most go on to high school. There are public schools and private schools. All Turkish children study a foreign language at school as well as Turkish, math, science, and history. At the end of high school, all students take a test. The score from this one test decides which subjects they can study for a degree and which college they can attend.

Hospitality

Turks have a famous tradition of hospitality, not only to friends and family but also toward strangers. Even shopkeepers insist that shoppers drink tea before beginning to talk about what they are seeking. Some people believe that this ancient tradition has its roots in religion.

Turks often invite visitors to their homes. When the visitor arrives, he or she is offered a pair of slippers to replace outdoor shoes. It is almost impossible for a guest to leave before accepting something to eat or drink. Juice, strong tea, and sweet coffee are the usual beverages. They are often served with something salty and something sweet to eat.

A lucky guest will be invited to stay for dinner. Turkish cuisine is world famous. A popular saying about Turkey is "Go for the history and stay for the food." Many dishes contain lamb, eggplant, or yogurt. One of the most popular dishes is kebab, grilled meat served with bread or rice, which is sold everywhere in fast-food restaurants called *kebabci*. Another popular food is

▲ A syrup seller pours a cup from a traditional metal tank on his back.

▼ Turkish delight, or *lokum*, is sold loose so people can choose their favorite flavors.

SPORTS FANS

The most popular sport in Turkey is soccer and fans are fiercely loyal to their local team. The best teams (Galatasary, Fenerbache, and Besitkas) regularly compete with the top teams across Europe. All three are based in Istanbul. Many Turkish players play in soccer leagues throughout Europe.

Another sport in which Turkey is a world leader is weightlifting. Turkish lifters regularly win gold medals at the Olympics.

One Turkish sport that is lesser known abroad is Turkish wrestling. Competitors dress in short leather trousers and cover their skin in oil. The oil makes it difficult for wrestlers to grip each other and knock their opponents down. The city of Edirne has hosted a wrestling competition every year since 1362, making it the world's oldest sports event.

▲ Every year swimmers race across the Bosporus from Europe to Asia.

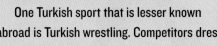

hamsi. This small fish from the Black Sea is called the "prince of fish." There are even songs and stories about it.

▼ **A chef cuts grilled meat in an Istanbul kebabci.**

Color and Sound

Turkey has a long tradition of cultural achievement. Under the Ottomans, poetry and architecture were both highly prized. Other artistic creations were carpets and rugs with complex, colorful designs woven from wool or silk, and handmade decorated tiles, which were widely used both inside and outside mosques.

Turks also have a rich musical tradition. When Ottoman armies went into battle, they took a marching band to intimidate their opponents, complete with loud drums. Today, the streets are often full of the sounds of the latest American, European, or Turkish pop artists. Traditional music is still popular, however. Many poets have written about the haunting sound of the *ney*, a flute that is still used in some Turkish music. The *oud* is a stringed instrument like a guitar with a round back. For centuries, people in Anatolia and Turkish speakers outside Anatolia made melodies with these instruments. Modern Turkish musicians use these old instruments to compose new music that straddles centuries.

▲ The Topkapi Palace in Istanbul is the largest example of Ottoman architecture. The bewildering network of courtyards, hallways, and towers was the sultan's home. It also housed his government, included a school, and held the harem—where the sultan's many wives and children lived.

◀ A musician plays a traditional long-necked lute called a *baglama saz*, which is the most common traditional stringed instrument in Turkey.

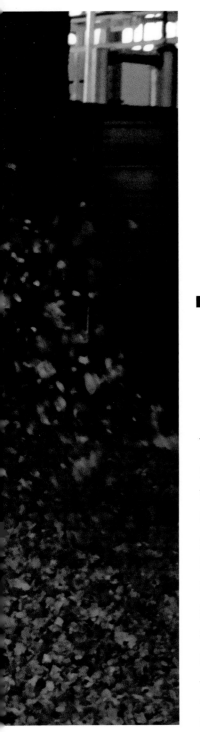

Ancient
but
Modern

TURKEY HAS THE 17TH-LARGEST economy in the world. Its supplies of iron support a large car-manufacturing industry; its cotton harvest makes it a leading producer of textiles. A less important but distinctive resource is flowers. Turkey is a major exporter of rose oil, which is used in perfumes, cosmetics, and alternative medicines. Rose water, which is flavored with rose petals, is used in one of Turkey's most famous foods: Turkish delight. This gel-like candy was first made in the Ottoman Empire 500 years ago. Today's economy is highly modernized. In 2006, Turkey joined with Azerbaijan and Georgia to build a 1,099-mile (1,768 km) oil pipeline from the Caspian Sea to the Turkish port of Ceyhan. The project helped supply Turkey's growing energy needs.

◀ A worker shovels rose petals in a factory making rose water and oil. The rose products are used in perfumes and as flavorings for candy.

GOVERNMENT AND RELIGION

Turks call Atatürk's political ideas Kemalism, and many Turks still wish the Turkish Republic to stay close to the Kemalist principles on which it was founded. In 1923, Atatürk insisted that the new Republic of Turkey must be a secular state. Although the state controls the country's religious institutions through the Religious Affairs General Directorate, the Turkish constitution does not allow religion to influence the government. No political party may have a formal connection with religion. The government is forbidden to introduce religious principles to the way in which it runs the country. In elections in 2007, Turks strongly supported the AK Party, which campaigned on a platform of bringing tolerance, liberal market policies, and honesty into the way government is run.

Trading Partners

Turkey's foreign trade has continued to grow in recent years. The country currently imports more than it exports. Automobiles and car parts lead the list of exports, with iron, steel, and various kinds of other mechanical equipment close behind. Turkey imports many raw materials used in factories and most of its fuel.

Country	Percent Turkey exports
European Union	51.7%
United States	5.9%
Russia	3.8%
Iraq	3.0%
All others combined	35.6%

Country	Percent Turkey imports
European Union	39.8%
Russia	12.9%
China	7.1%
United States	4.4%
All others combined	35.8%

▼ Muslim women are not forced to wear headscarves in Turkey, although young women are increasingly choosing to wear them.

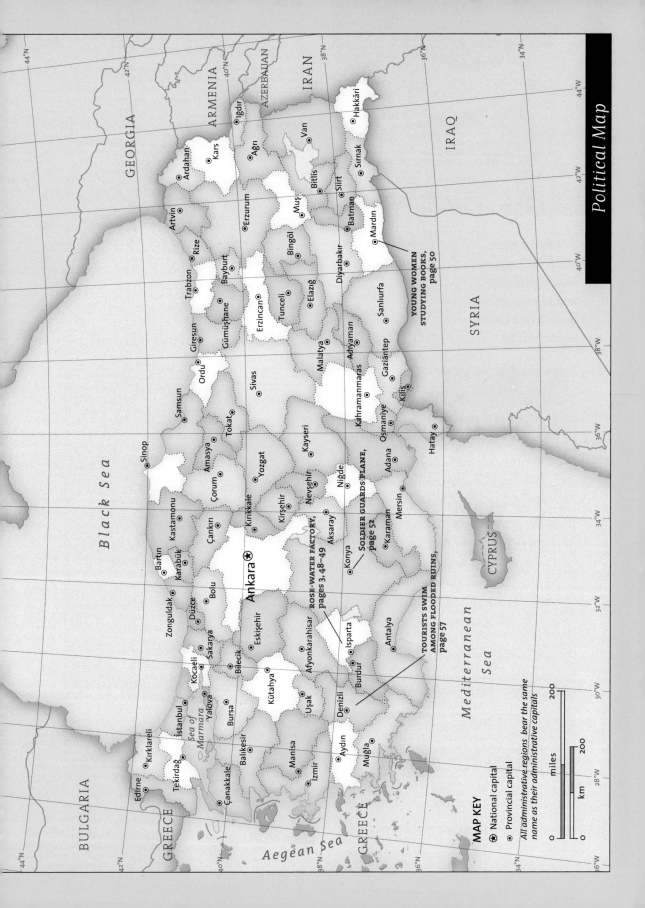

Political Map

BULGARIA

GREECE

GEORGIA

ARMENIA

AZERBAIJAN

IRAN

IRAQ

SYRIA

Black Sea

Sea of Marmara

Aegean Sea

Mediterranean Sea

CYPRUS

Edirne
Kırklareli
Tekirdağ
İstanbul
Yalova
Çanakkale
Kocaeli
Sakarya
Bilecik
Bursa
Balıkesir
Manisa
İzmir
Aydın
Muğla
Denizli
Uşak
Kütahya
Eskişehir
Bolu
Düzce
Zonguldak
Karabük
Bartın
Kastamonu
Sinop
Çankırı
Kırıkkale
Ankara
Afyonkarahisar
Isparta
Burdur
Antalya
Konya
Karaman
Mersin
Adana
Niğde
Aksaray
Nevşehir
Kırşehir
Yozgat
Çorum
Amasya
Samsun
Ordu
Giresun
Tokat
Sivas
Kayseri
Kahramanmaraş
Osmaniye
Hatay
Kilis
Gaziantep
Adıyaman
Malatya
Şanlıurfa
Elazığ
Tunceli
Erzincan
Gümüşhane
Trabzon
Bayburt
Rize
Artvin
Ardahan
Kars
Erzurum
Bingöl
Muş
Diyarbakır
Batman
Mardin
Siirt
Bitlis
Van
Ağrı
Iğdır
Hakkâri
Şırnak

YOUNG WOMEN STUDYING BOOKS, page 50

ROSE-WATER FACTORY, pages 3, 48–49

SOLDIER GUARDS PLANE, page 52

TOURISTS SWIM AMONG FLOODED RUINS, page 57

MAP KEY
✪ National capital
◉ Provincial capital
All administrative regions bear the same name as their administrative capitals

miles   200
km   200

Positions of Power

Turkey is one of the few democratic nations in the Muslim world and that makes it a valuable member of the North Atlantic Treaty Organization (NATO) defense alliance. Turkey is a neighbor of Iraq, Iran, and Syria—three nations that often express distrust of Western ideas and values. That makes it strategically important in world affairs.

The Turks continue to face important issues. In the 80 years since the Turkish Republic was established,

HOW THE GOVERNMENT WORKS

Turkey has both a head of government (the prime minister) and a head of state (the president). The prime minister is in charge of the country and is helped by a Council of Ministers. The president's role is mainly ceremonial; he or she represents the Turkish people on state visits. The president is elected for a 7-year term by the 550 members of the Grand National Assembly. These members are elected by all Turks over age 18 for 5-year terms. The political party that wins the most seats in the assembly forms a government, and its leader becomes the prime minister. Turkey's courts are independent of the other two branches of government. There are several types of courts in Turkey, including a Constitutional Court and a High Court of Appeals. All cases are decided by judges, not juries.

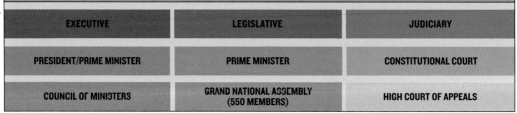

STRUCTURE OF THE STATE

EXECUTIVE	LEGISLATIVE	JUDICIARY
PRESIDENT/PRIME MINISTER	PRIME MINISTER	CONSTITUTIONAL COURT
COUNCIL OF MINISTERS	GRAND NATIONAL ASSEMBLY (550 MEMBERS)	HIGH COURT OF APPEALS

MINORITY VOICES

The Ottoman Empire brought together people from throughout the region, and modern Turkey still has many minorities. They include Kurds, who make up about 20 percent of people living in Turkey, along with Roma, Christians, Jews, Alevi, Bulgarians, Greeks, Armenians, Assyrians, Arabs, and Laz. Under the constitution, they are all Turkish citizens and they all have the same rights as other Turks. However, there is sometimes tension among Turkey's many cultures. Minority religious and ethnic groups suffer from intolerance. There have been attacks on Christians, for example. Many Turks believe that more should be done to prevent violence against minority groups and to improve human rights. As Turkey prepares for entry into the European Union, human rights may improve for all Turks.

▲ Kurds girls take part in a traditional wedding. About a fifth of Turkey's population are Kurds.

there have been four military coups. The army last seized power in 1980 to stop violence erupting over political disagreements. Each time, the army has tried to create stability. The Turks are now working on a new constitution that they hope will improve the freedom, prosperity, and civil rights they want.

Threats to Peace

Turkey faces other challenges, too. Among them are the group of Kurds who want to establish their own Kurdish homeland.

Another potential challenge is the tension between Turks who want a more liberal and tolerant

EUROPE: IN OR OUT?

Turkey became an associate member of the European Economic Community in 1963, but it was only in 2005 that talks began that might lead to full membership in the European Union (EU). Turkey already trades widely with members of the European Union. Full membership would allow Turks to live wherever they wanted within the EU. Some current EU members are worried that too many Turkish workers would come to their countries and take jobs. Some Turks want the benefits of EU membership. It would ensure the civil rights of everyone living in Turkey—something many Turks worry about now. The economic benefits could also raise Turkish living standards. However, other Turks do not like the idea of joining the EU. They say foreign countries would have too much control over Turkish society.

▲ The Turkish flag flies outside the European Council in Brussels.

government and those who believe that the country should remain as it is. In 2007, the Justice and Development (AK) Party, a moderate rightist party, was re-elected by an overwhelming majority. It ran on a platform of anticorruption, sound economic policies, and continuing the process toward European Union membership. The prime minister was from the AK Party, according to parliamentary procedure. The president, who is elected by the parliament, was also from the AK Party, as it had a clear majority.

A third problem is one faced by many countries: terrorist attacks. Both Kurdish and Islamist terrorists have planted bombs in Istanbul and other cities in the last two decades. They have killed thousands of military and civilian victims.

The final challenge is economic. Despite its resources, Turkey has been unable to provide all of its citizens with a high standard of living. This is partly because Turkey relies on exports to make money. That makes it vulnerable to changes in the world economy.

Rich Resources

Turkey once boasted that it was one of the few countries that could produce enough food to feed its whole population. Today, it both imports and exports food. Farmers rely on a wide range of farmland to grow different crops. Nuts are an important export crop; so are grains, vegetables, and dried apricots.

NUTS ABOUT NUTS

Anatolians have been growing and harvesting hazelnuts for thousands of years. Villagers on the Black Sea coast plant clumps of hazelnut bushes on rocky hills. Grazing goats keep the weeds down. Women and children pick the nuts when they ripen. Despite the lack of farming machinery, Turkey is the world's largest exporter of hazelnuts (pictured). Every year, it grows at least 70 percent of all of the world's hazelnuts. Turkey is also a leading producer of almonds (grown on the Aegean coast), pistachios (from the dry areas in the south), walnuts, and chestnuts. Turkey exported 12 percent of all of the world's tree nuts in 2003; only the United States exported more. Turks also eat many nuts, often as part of pastries. One special dessert is candied walnuts. Even the shell is sweet and edible.

INDUSTRY

Turkey's industrial zones are located on the coast of the Sea of Marmara, around Izmir and Adana, and in the suburbs of Ankara. Turkey is the largest steel producer in the Middle East. Its biggest steelworks are at Karabük.

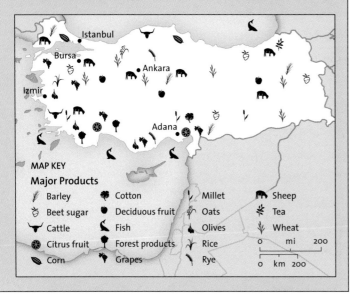

MAP KEY

Major Products

Barley	Cotton	Millet	Sheep
Beet sugar	Deciduous fruit	Oats	Tea
Cattle	Fish	Olives	Wheat
Citrus fruit	Forest products	Rice	
Corn	Grapes	Rye	

0   mi   200

0   km   200

▼ The leaders of Turkey, Georgia, and Azerbaijan celebrate the construction of an oil pipeline across their countries.

Among Turkey's most valuable resources are its rivers. The Southeastern Anatolian Project, known as GAP, has built 22 dams on the Euphrates and Tigris rivers. The dams provide water for land that would otherwise be too dry to farm. The government has also built 19 hydroelectric power plants to generate electricity from the dams.

Water Disputes

GAP aims to improve the whole region by supporting better education and economic development. Southeast Anatolia is now Turkey's leading cotton-growing area. Many towns in the area are growing into industrial centers. The dams are the most controversial GAP projects. The Euphrates and Tigris provide water to Turkey's neighbors, Syria and Iraq. Those countries complain that they are not getting enough water. Each year, Turkey and its neighbors resolve the problems by diplomatic negotiation.

Growing Economy

Turkey's economic growth has had positives and negatives. In the 1980s and early 1990s prices rose so quickly that money became nearly worthless. In 2001 the government introduced a new currency, YTL, or Yeni (new) Turkish Lira to try to stabilize prices. The economy improved. Turkey now exports many cars. Other major exports include cloth, clothing, steel, and medicines.

Turkey's tourist industry has also grown. Visitors come to see its ancient sites or to enjoy its beaches. People from throughout the Middle East visit to shop. The Cevahir Mall in Istanbul is the largest mall in Europe and the sixth largest in the world.

For the latest time in its long history, Turkey is acting as a bridge between the east and west, from Europe to Asia. Turkey will likely play a major part as key transportation and communication routes for the Balkans, Central Asia, and southwest Asia continue to develop and link up with the global economy.

▲ Visitors to Hierapolis share a hot spring with toppled columns from the town's ancient past. Hierapolis has been attracting visitors to the spa since the second century B.C.

Add a Little Extra to Your Country Report!

If you are assigned to write a report about Turkey, you'll want to include basic information about the country, of course. The Fast Facts chart on page 8 will give you a good start. The rest of the book will give you the details you need to create a full and up-to-date paper or PowerPoint presentation. But what can you do to make your report more fun than anyone else's? If you use your imagination and dig a bit deeper into some of the topics introduced in this book, you're sure to come up with information that will make your report unique!

>Flag

Perhaps you could explain the history of Turkey's flag, and the meanings of its colors and symbols. Go to **www.crwflags.com/fotw/flags** for more information.

>National Anthem

How about downloading Turkey's national anthem and playing it for your class? At **www.nationalanthems.info** you'll find what you need, including the words to the anthem and sheet music for the anthem. Simply pick "T" and then "Turkey" from the list on the left-hand side of the screen, and you're on your way.

>Time Difference

If you want to understand the time difference between Turkey and where you are, this Web site can help: **www.worldtimeserver.com**. Just click on "Current Times" and pick "Turkey" from the list on the right. If you called someone in Turkey right now, would you wake them up from their sleep?

>Currency

Another Web site will convert your money into lira, the currency used in Turkey. You'll want to know how much money to bring if you're ever lucky enough to travel to Turkey: **www.xe.com/ucc**.

>Weather

Why not check the current weather in Turkey? It's easy—go to **www.weather.com** to find out if it's sunny or cloudy, warm or cold in Turkey right now! Pick "World" from the headings at the top of the page. Then search for a Turkish city such as Istanbul or Ankara. The weather report will include temperature, humidity, wind, and time of sunrise and sunset. Scroll down the page for the 36-Hour Forecast and a satellite weather map. Compare your weather to the weather in the Turkish city you chose. Is this a good season, weather-wise, for a person to travel to Turkey?

>Miscellaneous

Still want more information? Simply go to National Geographic's World Atlas for Young Explorers at **http://www.nationalgeographic.com/kids-world-atlas**. It will help you find maps, photos, music, games, and other features that you can use to jazz up your report.

Glossary

Apostles followers of Jesus Christ. Several apostles preached in Turkey.

Archaeologist a person who looks for the remains of ancient civilizations and uses them to figure out how people lived in the distant past.

Architecture the style used to construct and decorate a building.

Calcium metal that commonly occurs as part of rocks, including chalk and limestone.

Climate the average weather of a certain place at different times of year.

Culture a collection of beliefs, traditions, and styles that belongs to people living in a certain part of the world.

Currency the money used in a country, such as dollars or pesos. Turkey's currency is lira.

Democracy a country that is ruled by a government chosen by all its people through elections.

Economy the system by which a country creates wealth through making and trading products.

Endangered an animal or plant that is at risk of dying out.

Ethnic group a group of people that come originally from a certain place and share the same culture.

Exported transported and sold outside the country of origin.

Fault a crack or opening in Earth's crust. The rocks on either side of the fault often move.

Fertile capable of supporting new life.

Imported brought into the country from abroad.

Judiciary the branch of the government that controls the courts and justice system.

Mineral a naturally occurring chemical.

Nomadic having no fixed home and frequently moving from place to place.

Peninsula a strip of land that is surrounded by water on three sides. The word comes from the Latin for "almost an island." The mainland of Turkey is a large peninsula.

Plateau a flat part of land that is high above sea level, as opposed to a plain, which is near to sea level. The western and central parts of Turkey are a plateau.

Province a region within a country that has some degree of control over its affairs.

Republic a country that is headed by an elected president.

Revolution a rapid, often violent, change of government when a large number of the country's people attack the government.

Richter Scale a system used to measure the strength of earthquakes. The scale runs from 1 to 9. An increase of 1 in the scale indicates a 10-fold increase in the energy released by the quake.

Sect a small religious group.

Secular based on worldly concerns, rather than on religious belief.

Species a type of organism. Animals or plants in the same species look similar and can only breed successfully among themselves.

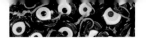

Bibliography

Alexander, Vimala. *Welcome to Turkey*. Milwaukee, WI: Gareth Stevens Publishing, 2002.

Blomquist, Christopher. *A Primary Source Guide to Turkey*. New York, NY: PowerKids Press, 2005.

Harmon, Daniel E. *Turkey*. Philadelphia, PA: Mason Crest Publishers, 2004.

http://www.tccb.gov.tr/pages/ president (official Web site of Turkish president)

http://news.bbc.co.uk/1/hi/ world/europe/country_ profiles/1022222.stm (general information)

http://www.state.gov/r/pa/ei/ bgn/3432.htm (general information)

Further Information

NATIONAL GEOGRAPHIC Articles

Gore, Rick. "Istanbul on Edge." NATIONAL GEOGRAPHIC (October 2002): 112-133.

Web sites to explore

More fast facts about Turkey, from the CIA (Central Intelligence Agency): https://www.cia.gov/library/ publications/the-world- factbook/geos/tu.html

Take a virtual tour of Turkey's presidential villa in Ankara: http://www.tccb.gov.tr/common /sanaltur/eng/index.html

The father of modern Turkey, Atatürk was the first president of the republic in the 1920s. Find out more about his life, watch videos of him, and read the biographies of other Turkish presidents at http://www.tccb.gov.tr/pages/ ata_special/Biography/

Turkey is a huge country filled with many beautiful landscapes and historical sites. This inter- active map is a good place to start finding out about them: http://www.goturkey.com/map. php?from=1&lng=en#. Links to further information appear on the right beside the list of cities.

Çatal Höyük is one of the oldest towns ever discovered. Work on the 8,800-year-old buildings is still going on. Find out the latest at http://www.catalhoyuk.com

Learn more about Ephesus, one of the greatest cities of the ancient Mediterranean, at http://www.ephesusturkey.de/ panorama. Click on each of the numbers to get a better view of the ruined city. Istanbul has some of the largest and most splendid mosques in the world. Get a 360° view of the city's

Bayezid Mosque at http://www.panoramas.dk/ fullscreen6/f11-istanbul.html

See, hear

There are many ways to get a taste of life in Turkey, such as movies and music. You might be able to locate these:

Topkapi (1964)
An enjoyable family film about a daring jewel robbery from the high-security vault of Istanbul's Topkapi Palace.

Turkish Daily News
Read what is making the headlines today in Turkey at http://www.turkishdailynews. com.tr

Index

Boldface indicates illustrations.

Adapazari, earthquake damage **12**
Aegean Sea 11, 14
    beach **10**
AK Party 50, 54
Alevis 43
Alexander the Great 28-29
Anatolia 13, **13**, 14, 18, 26, 28, 29,
    31, 33, 34, 40
Anatolian shepherd dog *see*
    kangal
ancient civilizations 10, 11, 18, 25,
    25, 26
Ankara **13**, 32
Antiochus I **28**
Anzac Cove **34**
Ararat, Mount 15, **15**
archaeology 13, **25**
architecture, Ottoman 33–34, 42,
    42, **47**
area 8, 13
Asia 10, 25
Asia Minor, province 29
Atatürk, Kemal 34, 35, **35**, 40
Atatürk Dam **14**

baglama saz **47**
beverages 45, **45**
Bird Lake 17, **17**
birds, species 17
Black Sea 8, 10, **10**, 11, 46
Blue Mosque 42, **42**
Bodrum, castle **31**
Bosporus 11, **11**, 12, 13, 23, 30,
    40
    bridges 13
    rail tunnel 13
    swimming race **46**
Bulgaria 12
Byzantine Empire 30
    Muslim attacks 32
Byzantium 30, 32

camels **22**
capital 8, 32
Cappadocia **13**, 30, **30**
carpets and rugs 46
Çatal Höyük 25, **25**
Cevahir Mall 57
Ceyhan 49

Christianity 29, 30
cities 38
climate 8
clothes 41
coinage 28
constitution 53
Constantine, emperor 29–30, 32
Constantinople 30, 32, **32**
    fall of 33
    see also Istanbul
cotton 56
Cotton Castle *see* Pamukkale
coups, military 35, 53
Croesus 28
crops, cotton 56
Crusaders 32
    castle **31**
currency 8, 57

dams **14**, 15, 55, 56
Dardanelles 11, 12
democracy 35, 52
dervishes 43, **43**
devshirme 34
dolphins 23

earthquakes 12, **12**
Eastern Anatolian Highlands 15
economy 49
    challenges 54-55
    growth 57
Edirne 46
electricity **14**, 15, 56
Ephesus 29
    Great Theater **29**
Euphrates River **14**, 15, 55, 56
Euro 2008 37, **37**
Europe 10, 25
European Union 37, 54
exports 50, 55, 57

family 44
farming 14, 20
    origins 18
fish 22–23
    Black Sea 10
    hamsi 46
    turbot **23**
fishing **17**
flowers 22, **22**
food 45, 55

forest cat **21**
forests 20, 21

Galata Tower **33**
Gallipoli 11, **34**, 35
GAP 56
Germany, guest workers 37
Giresun **10**
goats **21**
Golden Horn **5**, 23
government 50, 52
Grand National Assembly 52
Greece 12
    ancient 11, 28

headscarves 42, **50**
Hierapolis **57**
Hissarlik 26
Hittites 26, 28
holidays, national 41
Homer 26
hospitality 45

imports 50
industry 49, 56
    map **56**
instruments, musical 47, **47**
invasions 29
Islam 31, 42, 50
Istanbul 11, 12, 32, 33, 44, 46
    Blue Mosque **42**
    Bogazici University **41**
    Bosporus **11**, 40
    Cevahir Mall 57
    dolphins 23
    Galata Tower **33**
    kebabci **46**
    name 30
    Topkapi Palace **47**
Italians **33**
Izmit 12
Iznik 42

Jalal al-Din Rumi (Mevlana) 43
Jesus 29
Jews 43-44

kangal 20, **20**
kebab 45, **46**
Kemalism 50
Knights Hospitaller **31**

Kurds 14, 53, **53**
Kus Golu 17, **17**

lakes 8, 22
  Bird Lake 17, **17**
  Lake Van 15
languages 8, 14, 38, 40, 41, 44
  Turkish phrases 38
learning 31, 33
location 11, 25, 52
Lydia 28

malaria 56
maps
  climate zones **8**
  historical **27**
  industry **56**
  physical **9**
  political **51**
  population **39**
  vegetation and ecosystems **19**
Mediterranean Sea 11
Mevlevi sect *see* dervishes
Midas 28
mosques 34, 42, **42**
Mount Nemrut **28**
mountains 8, 14
  Eastern Anatolian Highlands 14
  Taurus 14
music 47
Mustafa Kemal *see* Atatürk, Kemal
myths 15, 28

name, official 8
national parks 18, 23
neighbors 8, 12, 52, 56
ney 47
Noah, bible story 15
Nobel Prize 44
nomads **38**
North Anatolian Fault 12
North Atlantic Treaty Organization
  (NATO) 52, **52**
nuts 55, **55**

obsidian **25**
oil pipeline 49, **56**
Olüdeniz **10**
Orthodox Church 30, 43
Osman 33
Osmanlis *see* Ottomans

Ottomans 32, 33
  architecture 33–34, 42, **42**, **47**
  army 34, 47
  devshirme 34
  empire 33, 41
  Süleyman I **33**
oud 47

Pactolus River 28
Pamuk, Orhan 44, **44**
Pamukkale 7, **7**
Paul, apostle 29
Persia 11
  empire 23
Phrygia 28
population 8
  ancestors 41
  ethnic minorities 53
  urban and rural 38
position, strategic 52, 57

Ramadan 41
refugees, Greek and Armenian 35
religion 42–43, 50
  and government 50, 53
Republic of Turkey 35
resources 38, 49, 55
rivers 8, 55
Romans 7
  Roman Empire 11, 29, 30
roses 22, **22**
  rose water 49, **49**

schools 44
Sea of Mamara 11, 12
secularism 35, 50
Seljuks 31, 32
  empire 31
  fall 32
settlers
  early 40
  Muslim 31
shipping 11
Sinan 33
size 13
soccer 37, **37**, 46
Southeastern Anatolian Project
  (GAP) 55
sports 37, 46
steel 56
steppe 20

students, university **41**
Süleyman I **33**
Süleyman Mosque 34
Sultan Ahmet Mosque *see* Blue
  Mosque

Taurus Mountains 15, 22
terrorism 54
Tigris River 15, 55, 56
tile-making 42, 46
time line 26
Topkapi Palace **47**
tourism 7, 57, **57**
trade routes 11
trading partners 50
trees, species 21
Trojan War 26
Troy 26
  wooden horse **26**
tulips, origins 22
turbot **23**
Turkey Red, wheat 18
Turkish delight **45**, 49
Turkish War of Independence
  34-35
Turkish wrestling 46
Turks, definition 40

Van, Lake, 15
vegetation zones 18
volcanoes 15

water, usage 56
weightlifting 46
wheat, Turkey Red 18
wildflowers 18
wildlife
  at risk 18
  loggerhead turtles 23
  marine life 22
  Mediterranean monk seal 23
  northern bald ibis **18**
  pelicans **17**
  species 17, 21
  tigers 21
  Turkish horned viper **23**
  wolves 20
World War I 34, **34**

Yazili Park 23

Credits

Picture Credits

Front Cover – Spine Robert Paul van Beets/Shutterstock; Top: Blaine Harrington/Corbis; Low Far Left: Jonathan Blair/NGIC; Low Left: Bruno Ehrs /Corbis; Low Right: Faith Saribas/ Corbis; Low Far Right: Martin Gray/NGIC.

Interior – Alamy: Images & Stories: 2–3, 24–25; Corbis: Lynsey Addario: 41 lo, 44 up; Dave Bartfruff: 46 lo; Yann Arthus-Bertrand: 47 up; Patrick Frilet: 2; Rose Hartman: 21 lo; Chris Hellier: 18; Hemis: 11 up; Dave G. Houser: 35 up; Hulton Deutsch Collection: 34 up; Karen Hunt: 29 up; Catherine Ivill: 4 left, 36–37; Gavriel Jecan: 28 lo; Wolfgang Kaehler: 47 lo; Lawrence Manning: 5 up; Joe McDonald: 23 lo; Reuters: 52 up; Thierry Roge: 54 up; Faith Saribas: 3 right, 16–17, 46 up; Marco Simon/Robert Harding: 10 up; Herbert Spichtinger/zefa: 42 lo; David Sutherland: 45 up; Murat Taner/Zefa: 13 lo; Arthur Thevenart: 4 right, 22 up, 48–49; David Turnley: 53 lo; Peter Turnley: 40 up; Terry Whittaker/FLPA: 21 up; Adam Woolfitt: 23 up; Getty Images: Istockphotos: 55, 59; Mustafa Ozer: 56 lo; Steve Satushek/Image Bank: 3 left, 5–6, 20 lo; NGIC: Jonathan Blair: 30 up; David Boyer: 22 lo; Gordon Gahan: 15 up, 31 lo; Jean-Leon Huens: 32 up; Ed Kashi: 14 lo; Manoocher: 13 up, 50; Steve McCurry: 33 lo, 45 lo; Robert Moore: 10 lo; Randy Olson: 14 up; Reza: 12 up, 57; James L Stanfield: 26, 33 up, 38 lo left, 43 up;

Text copyright © 2009 National Geographic Society
Published by the National Geographic Society.
All rights reserved. Reproduction of the whole or any part of the contents without written permission from the National Geographic Society is strictly prohibited.

For information about special discounts for bulk purchases, contact National Geographic Special Sales: ngspecsales@ngs.org

For more information, please call 1-800-NGS-LINE (647-5463) or write to the following address:

NATIONAL GEOGRAPHIC SOCIETY
1145 17th Street N.W.
Washington, D.C. 20036-4688 U.S.A.

Visit us online at www.nationalgeographic.com/books

Library of Congress Cataloging-in-Publication Data available on request
ISBN: 978-1-4263-0387-6

Printed in the United States of America

Series design by Jim Hiscott.
The body text is set in Avenir; Knockout.
The display text is set in Matrix Script.

Front Cover—Top: Grand Bazaar, Istanbul; Low Far Left: Family and donkey climbing a hill in Cappadocia; Low Left: Turkish delight; Low Right: Pelicans at Manyas Lake in northwestern Turkey; Low Far Right: Stone head at Nemrut Dag archaeological site

Page 1—Bathers on Olüdeniz Beach; Icon image on spine. Contents page, and throughout: Tiles

Produced through the worldwide resources of the National Geographic Society

John M. Fahey, Jr., *President and Chief Executive Officer*; Gilbert M. Grosvenor, *Chairman of the Board*; Tim T. Kelly, *President, Global Media Group*; John Q. Griffin, *President, Publishing*; Nina D. Hoffman, *Executive Vice President, President of Book Publishing Group*

National Geographic Staff for this Book

Nancy Laties Feresten, *Vice President, Editor-in-Chief of Children's Books*
Bea Jackson, *Director of Design and Illustration*
Jim Hiscott, *Art Director*
Virginia Koeth, Rebecca Baines, *Project Editors*
Lori Epstein, *Illustrations Editor*
Grace Hill, *Associate Manging Editor*
Stacy Gold, Nadia Hughes, *Illustrations Research Editors*
R. Gary Colbert, *Production Director*
Lewis R. Bassford, *Production Manager*
Nicole Elliott, *Manufacturing Manager*
Mapping Specialists, Ltd., *Maps*

Brown Reference Group plc. Staff for this Book

Volume Editor: Tom Jackson
Designer: Dave Allen
Picture Manager: Sophie Mortimer
Maps: Martin Darlison
Artwork: Darren Awuah
Index: Kay Ollerenshaw
Senior Managing Editor: Tim Cooke
Children's Publisher: Anne O'Daly
Editorial Director: Lindsey Lowe

About the Author

SARAH SHIELDS is a professor of history at the University of North Carolina, Chapel Hill. She is currently researching the development of national identities in the Middle East between the two world wars. She has two children who have gotten used to traveling with her on research trips.

About the Consultants

DR. MICHAEL MCADAMS is presently an assistant professor in the Geography Department at Fatih University in Istanbul, Turkey. His recent articles have concentrated on fractal analysis of cities, Geographic Information Science education, the use of Remote Sensing in archaeology, Southeast Europe transportation intergration, global cultural centers, and Bus Rapid Transit Systems. He has extensive knowledge of the geography and social conditions in Turkey and has used Istanbul and Southeast Europe as a focus for much of his recent research.

ALLISON HART is a research assistant in the Foreign Policy Program at the Brookings Institution in Washington, D.C. Her research focuses on political and social dynamics in Europe and the greater Middle East and U.S. policy toward these regions. She recently completed work on Philip Gordon and Omer Taspinar's *Winning Turkey: How America, Europe, and Turkey Can Revive a Fading Partnership* (Brookings, 2008). Her academic background is in Middle East language and civilization, which she studied at Northwestern University.

Time Line of
Turkish History

B.C.

ca 6800 Ancient people build one of the world's earliest settlements at Çatal Höyük.

ca 1700 The Hittites establish an empire centered in Anatolia.

ca 1100 The Hittite empire declines; various kingdoms arise in its place

ca 700 King Midas rules Phrygia in western Turkey.

334 Alexander the Great brings Anatolia under Macedonian Greek rule.

129 Anatolia becomes part of the Roman province of Asia Minor.

A.D.

330 The Roman emperor Constantine builds a new capital in the east: Constantinople.

ca 550 The Byzantine Empire reaches its maximum extent under Justinian I.

ca 650 Islam gains popularity in neighboring Armenia.

ca 900 Powerful Armenian families establish independent kingdoms throughout modern-day Turkey.

1000

1071 Seljuk forces defeat the Byzantine army at the Battle of Manzikert, leading to the conquest of Anatolia by Turkic tribes.

1096 Christian Crusaders on their way to the Holy Land capture modern-day Iznik and force the Seljuks to find a new capital.

1200

1204 Christian armies on the Fourth Crusade overthrow the Byzantine Empire.

1243 The Mongol dynasty of Iran defeat the Seljuks at the Battle of Köse Dagh; Iranian influence and power spreads throughout Anatolia.

1261 Michael VIII Palaiologos regains control of Constantinople and reestablishes the Byzantine Empire.

1299 Osman declares a kingdom independent of the Seljuk Empire; it will become the Ottoman Empire

1400

1453 Ottoman forces conquer the Byzantine capital at Constantinople, modern-day Istanbul.

1500

1512 Selim I comes to the throne; he will expand the empire to include Egypt, Syria, and the holy cities of Mecca and Medina in Arabia.

1520 Süleyman I becomes sultan; in his 46-year reign, he expands the boundaries of the empire into modern Hungary, Georgia, Iran, and Iraq.

1600

1683 Ottoman forces are defeated by Polish–Lithuanian and Hapsburg troops at the Battle of Vienna.

1727 Ibrahim Müteferrika founds the first printing press for works in Arabic, Persian, and Turkish in Istanbul.